COMING TO THIS

COMING TO THIS

poems by

Joanne Lowery

FITHIAN PRESS ❖ SANTA BARBARA ❖ 1990

ACKNOWLEDGMENTS

"Breathing on Mirrors"	*Manhattan Poetry Review*
"God"	*Manhattan Poetry Review*
"Wishbones"	*Crosscurrents*
"Walking in the Rain"	*Spoon River Quarterly*
"Color January"	*Spoon River Quarterly*
"Pink Dog"	*The Reaper*
"The First Little Pig"	*Crab Creek Review*
"Mauve"	*Northland Quarterly*
"Mirage"	*Northland Quarterly*
"Angels"	*Piedmont Literary Review*
"How Long Is a Long Time"	*Manhattan Poetry Review*
"Lady Crane"	*Manhattan Poetry Review*
"May 30"	*The Wooster Review*
"The Nile"	*Galley Sail Review*
"Escape"	*Plainsongs*
"Nightfall"	*Spoon River Quarterly*
"In December"	*Roanoke Review*
"Two Clocks and So Forth"	*Mind in Motion*
"Grandma"	*Spoon River Quarterly*

LIBRARY OF CONGRESS CATALOGING-IN-PUBLICATION DATA
Lowery, Joanne, 1945-
Coming to this : poems / by Joanne Lowery
    p.   cm.
ISBN 0-931832-50-0 : $7.50
I. Title
PS 3562.0895c66 1990
811'.54—dc 20   90-2779 CIP

PUBLISHED BY FITHIAN PRESS
POST OFFICE BOX 1525
SANTA BARBARA, CALIFORNIA, 93102

For Alex

Contents

THIS

COMING TO THIS

GETTING STARTED

LITTLE LIVES

A tiny lady with a rosebud of a name
began for us Rosita's Restaurant,
which hasn't changed in a decade.
Today we are the only guests
as a jukebox plays slow guitar.
Outside, workmen are fixing the crumbly street
in a cloud of dust and sun.
Their tools rattle like castanets
while we eat what the student waitress
brought us from a generation ago.

Rosita, light once spilled from the door
of your pleasant Mexican cafe.
We came and left, we came back,
and each time we knew we'd left home.
The girl will wipe the checkered tablecloth clean
and scrape our empty plates into the sink.
Meanwhile, we drive the back roads
past see-through barns and farmyards
dotted with the leisurely blooms of peonies.
The land rolls up and down like flung cloth
until the town of our first choosing
disappears behind our backs. Rosita,
if we had known you, you would not
recognize us anymore when we enter.
Now we eat under your name without thinking.

WISHBONES

Against all reason I store onions
in a basket full of dried wishbones
until I forget they gather dust there.
To get to the heart of an onion
makes me cry peevishly,
and the wishbones remind me
how long I've been losing at luck.
I should try more often
to test the leverage of my thumb.

There's even the lyre-shaped bone
from a meal of duck I can't remember.
I am afraid to snap that one
in case a special wish splits
in the other person's favor.
It is such a small thing I ask,
that you tell me how life
feels on the other side
before I try again
to get this one yellow skin
to slip free of its root.
You are necessary even if
my fingers prove impossible,
and after all this time
I know you'll keep.

PINK DOG

His stage is a circle of printed snow
where he runs at chain's length.
His morning performance is lost,
the fate of a white dog.

In late afternoon someone unsnaps
the hook to give him a free show.
But his dance is circumscribed
by memory and pounded ice.

The sun which never moves
stays fixed to a second story window
like a gold sovereign retrieved
from some richer time.

The hills are mottled rose
the color of Italian marble,
the air blooms with petals
fallen from a western sun.

For his encore the dog leaps
into a suffusion of passing light
where he flies on gravity's tip:
a pink dog above pink snow.

TWO CLOCKS AND SO FORTH

In this room there are two clocks facing my repose.
The high one sits on a chest of drawers
rescued and carted from the Deep South
years ago when a day was just a day.

This clock was bought with dead love
and beats too fast, its silver pulse pushing
at its hands until they clap and sigh.

Another younger clock stays on grandma's table,
and though its turquoise wand counts each minute,
something gets lost within its flailing arms.

The two cannot agree.
They forever speak different minutes.

So when I look up, I always see the time between,
the part of my life that can never happen
or has somehow slipped on past.

Already I feel the threat of summer
when the air is pasted to skin
and the sun shrieks like a flaming trumpet
until I cannot move.

Day after day it will be noon
whichever way I turn my head.
The clocks will fidget, humming like gnats
unscreened around my head.

I will wait for them to line up

fold their spears, pray, say

we will be good now, you only
have to live your life this once
without synchrony.

GRANDMA

She lived in a shingle-sided gingerbread house
on a corner lot with a black iron gate.
She lived without love, lived to be old.
I am nothing like her, never will be.

Her breasts were so deep inside housedresses
that I never saw them, never knew if she was a woman
or just a mother in name, my mother
one of the products of her divided legs.

Her eyes were hooded and green as a parrot's,
and she spoke six languages unhappily.
When her husband died, we knew he left
on purpose to avoid her brown braid.

That's the story I believed about someone
whose stove looked like it could become a chicken
and whose smell would not wash away
in the blood of sweet Jesus.

Later I listened to her tell about the carriage
that drove through the village dust of her youth
before she came to this country, this country,
where misery was part of the Constitution.

She fell down the stairs, got mugged,
created feuds, counted great-grandchildren,
got smaller with every year and disappeared.
I am nothing like her, never will be.

If her womb and her daughter's and mine
were sliced and fit together into pear-shaped links,
then I could see some connection.
But I am too tall, and my hair shows early gray.

JUMPER

Failure hangs from his dry shoulders as he walks to the end
of the diving board on boneless feet, meat slapping.
Below him sharks laugh and a swim instructor beckons
You can do it, Now on the count of three.
His child-sized manhood retreats against his body:
at age seven, he already knows where courage lives
behind his shifting eyes. It is his decision to step off
and try to stand for a moment on top of air. One.
Resolve is just the seed of a person's greatness
like taking the dare to kiss a girl or end it all. Two.
Resolve turns away from the morning sun, then
suddenly breaks free from all there is to lose.
He knows he can do it, brain to leg, the electric step
to repeat the law of Newton's apple. Three.

The other children are gone. A cicada begins from a tree
at the far side of the pool, over the fence.
He feels what it is to be human, toes pointed
like pale morsels high above the water's head,
then thinks Now what? even as he falls
fast enough to escape the next panicky thought.
Cold lips pucker, suck, swallow him away,
until she reaches down and lifts him to the sun
as she will do the next time too. He was lucky
to live through it, hair sticking to his head, heart
beating like a frog as he struggles to the ladder,
up the edge, looking over his shoulder at what he has done.
In his eyes, one the color of water, the other blue as the sky,
he sees himself take a leap as if to die,
but by himself sink, drown, survive.

POEM FOR A DAUGHTER'S BIRTHDAY

She gets older every year after harvest
when the sky whitens like the belly of a dove
and the fields are finally cut low,
a girl taller to the eye
than a tree across the horizon
and as dark as an unnamed distant star.
From now on everything will be remembered,
surviving the confusion of childhood
as the time comes for her to walk up on stage
alone and find the words she wants to say.
Her heels click hello, her pockets giggle,
a fan of slender fingers pushes back her hair.
People who know her watch from the front
row as she steps into a cone of light.
It is not true that she is just now
beginning, only that from now on
like her eye's own pupil she opens
only to tighten back round herself,
looking at what no one else sees
while she takes in today.

THE CAT

After he planted a bald cypress down the hill
      with the other new trees,
I watch him bring the shovel up and stop
      to throw a ball to his son.
The window framed them, held them as they stood
      facing each other and the ball.
Then a white cat ran in between
      striking a pose of glazed porcelain.
It was after rain had fallen thick as paper
      and the grass wet my tiny feet.
I shook my head to scatter the spray
      from everything I had touched in the world:
this hillside I am forever walking up,
      and the boy who belongs to me,
the man with the shovel that belongs to him
      and the tree finding its new home.
I did not wave or flick my tail,
      I did not hold them tight
to the white flower of my breast
      dragging through the grass.
Let them play awhile until the winter snows
      and the trees forget their leaves.
I will watch them from this window,
      love pressed against the glass,
while darkness stumbles over the cat's sheen
      as they come up the rest of the hill.

SOME GEESE

Far from Canada, far from their other home, the geese gather
on the banks of this manmade pond, in no hurry
to leave despite the snows of early winter.
They stand like pebble-gray penguins on the ice
as if water and air were everything, food forgotten.
Some may join the ragged lines fleeing to the southeast,
but other geese, weary of battling the inner call to travel,
line up three abreast from a cloud of local residents
and glide close to the ground with the certainty of bombers.
Their cry is the same as if they had just returned from heaven,
had dipped their wings in celestial paint: graw graw,
graw, all honking the same urgent message, graw.
Forget the broad lakes of Alberta, forget the warm bayous,
leave your mate piercing the sky alone.
You are the only one like you the gaggle has ever known,
and this Midwestern beauty bares its flat breast
in the hope you will fly even lower, touch down, disobey.

THE PHEASANT

She walks through the low field where she lives
dressed like the bushes, the dusty grass that surrounds her.
Somewhere, eggs are waiting. It is spring wherever
she looks, northsoutheastwest, her tail a rudder
of contradiction, her tail a flat fan gone crazy
as she patrols what she calls her own.
The neighbor's cat follows her off to one side:
her eye is a seed where his shape continually grows.
He is the color of alchemy, he walks with half his legs
bent for the magician's trick, the field pulled away
quick as a tablecloth beneath her claws, his paws.
She is big enough for him to dance with
but looks too feathered for him to eat alone.
He stalks her like a bobbing bush, in love
with movement not his own, padding after her
in a trail of fear. They both will die,
it is just a matter of time, the field plowed away
into grass too green to hide in. Her shells
will lie broken like reminders of another time,
her bones discarded among snapped twigs.
The cat sleeps, dreaming of victory, how he scattered
her day back and forth out of its usual path,
until buoyed by a stiff wind she flew
low to the ground, honking her grief, masking her fear
with this blind excuse for song.

MAY 30

All this time I spent inside an old garage
prisoner and slave to May, the man
who makes me walk in circles like a dandelion
with its head blown off. Grass grows
through the gravel floor, dust motes quicken.
Standing on my toes, I get taller too,
polish my edges, stoke energy saved.
Rakes and a watering can grow old with me,
unneeded as the lawn sorts itself out
and early morning drops a shower.
Suddenly everything is ready. I had nothing
to do with it: nature, the world, life.
But now the month is over, or will be,
as flushed with summer's animal heat
I burst through the open-hinged doors
and race in an emerald Eldorado
chrome-streaming and cloud-splitting
straight down the street to June.

SINGING ON THE BACKSIDE OF THE MOON

ankle-deep in dust and rocks
I stand it's a little bit lonely.
out there The Universe is a sort of room
empty as this one.
listen, I will start to hum.
willows beaded with spring's first leaves
sway before me, grazing the stars.
spring and fall cut the year in half,
a flat white apple,
but here I can sing forever,
shadowless as a black cat
crossed out with ink.

my song is true and bad.
if I hide behind the moonman's
cheesy grin, it sounds safe.
wherever he goes, he faces away,
singing to the great distance
of heaven and an empty room.
no one answers, I do not die.
nor did I learn to love
by reading it in books,
write by being told to,
live because I must.

hunkered down, I taste the salt
blistering my knees.
another half year will spin
shut on the dark close of fall.
by then this song will hush
in the absence of wind,
persistent absence of lovers,
faint blur of human bells.

THE NILE

I find myself thinking openly of the Nile
half a world away and forever the same:
the black mud, the black hair, hyacinth and papyrus
together without shade from the sun.
Their distant flood repeats regular as a woman,
and from its sediment emerges something so sad
that it can only be called life, but not mine.
The pyramids don't matter either, or the pain
settling like flies wherever I am spared a look.

Here the grass grows green after last week's long rains,
and the trees are soaked from below by springs.
Nothing cataclysmic, worthy of note, spreading
like a dirty veil laced with crocodiles.
The days swim by sleek as fish,
and today while the sun pours and pours
outside where I am sitting, I think
about what I can dredge up from memory's silt
and rinse clean of disuse: desire
sitting on my lap like an old man,
a small thing alive in a big world.

NIGHTFALL

The lord of the second universe slips the sun
into an empty slot in the west,
buying for us another night.
Our golden coin, worn smooth by transactions
from millennia past, takes a long time to fall,
painfully pink, goading, goading. We didn't
ask please the price of rest, a wage for sleep.
Like everything else, it happens regardless.
We are driving inside a bubble of light
that races toward some perfect world
where love is free, and day hangs forever
without reproach, a white screen.

CLAMS

If you forget who you are, eat clams.
The sand will sit in your teeth,
reminiscent of faraway beaches.
You could be there and call it paradise,
never arguing with yourself
about whether life will ever be good.
The clams would belong there,
and probably you would too.

Instead, buy them in the open courtyards
of the area's newest supermarket.
The can is on a middle aisle,
bidding buy me, buy me.
You have always been eager to please,
and they are just babies,
stripped of their shells and sloshing
in juice not of their own making.
The sand is there to comfort them,
as it will later comfort you.

When you eat baby clams
and wash them down with wine,
that will answer your question:
for the moment the animal feeds.
With that assurance and the taste
of ocean lingering in your mouth,
it will take nothing more than faith
to follow when love
stoops to scoop you up
out of your own gray shell.

BECAUSE OF ANGELS

HOW LONG IS A LONG TIME

I cannot bring myself to say this:
you know I am afraid I love you.
The words rumble beneath our chairs
and we both are burning, burning.
Behind you through the enormous window
and our two stories down
a small lake opens before my eyes
like everything else I never knew was true.
I watch the lifespan of my words
take shape in your eyes;
who knows how long what I have said
will stay reflected there.
If only I could reverse the moment
and take back those few words
that banged like unruly children
on the trapdoor of my throat.
We can forget I ever said it.
The lake shrinks in the afternoon sun.
Perhaps you did not hear me
and still wait for me to speak:
tomorrow I might begin.

ANGELS

When you are ready
two angels will come to stay with you.
They will fall from heaven like ash,
passing through nothing,
passing through the gray glass of the sky.
They leave behind however many fathers
you happen to have
to take up residence on your shoulders.
Though you cannot see them
with eyes good enough to trace
the lifeline of your palm
they share the shape of men,
a bit slighter in the bone.
Nor do they have wings, wings
being the deranged creation
of medieval artists who didn't understand
flight apart from birds.
No, angels are the same as you or me,
of a finer sort, perhaps.
I wonder if I am one of yours
while you are one of mine
doing half the care,
half the proper steerage,
part of the continuous intercession
keeping us alive.

Or else I am nowhere near you,
wingless and alone, saying
I have wished for you
some divine companionship,
and that it is your deep abiding lack
which prevents your seeing their face
or mine, which weighs your hands
too heavy to clasp theirs
while I hover off somewhere
with cold white arms.

MAUVE

Only this early in the year with a crush of new snow
can I see afternoon lie down and die,
a landscape blue as an unwilling woman.
Pink lace hangs in the clouds
for as long as it takes to say pink lace,
then more from the west, rosy sheers,
autumn plum, the embarrassment of morning.
Suddenly I love you so much
that I would leave this place forever
and let someone else watch flesh darken to dusk.
All it takes is January, snow, and the four o'clock sun
for me to know my favorite color is
somewhere between purple and gray
and like you, close to gone.

SKIN

She calls me Small Woman, and still asleep
I wonder why, if I should have my bones shortened
to please her, be like her, or leave my clothes
behind and settle in nude splendor at her feet.
Awake I know I am not too tall, just old
by twenty years that were hers. Her skin
like honey-scented paper next to his.
When she scoffed, before she pushed my chest
so that I fell into the cold lap of morning,
she granted I knew a little about words.
Never enough. But from her dark-haired lecture
I gained no absolution, no poetry, no truth.

Tiny lady, she stands more comfortable than me.
I scratch, passion blistering my skin,
while she moves like magic day to day.
I wish for her—unknown as a corpse—
fat thighs, coarse manners, utter density.
Instead she is all that envy can supply,
and I am shrinking, thinking how much space
there is now that I hang in pieces
inside myself, all this skin slumped
to my ankles like an unwelcome gown.

COLOR JANUARY

Think of a child's coloring book, pages for every month.
We begin at the beginning.

The pages are manilla expanses with simple outlined shapes.
A woman on the left side.
A man on the right.

They are full of great spaces to color in.
Let us make her as blue as Mary
because of her deep-lidded eyes
and the tiny heart that blazes through her parka
almost igniting her scarf, her hair.

The man does not look at her because he does not know
if he is her twin or her lover, he is so many people
with a small heart of his own.
We can draw it in if we like,
an emblem of grace on an old black coat.

These pages are glued together into a seamed valley.
Our two people reach toward the center margins,
almost slide into the crevasse,
while at the same time holding tightly to the ropes of their
          sleds.
The ground is bruised with tracks, with mud and grass.
If we find some fresh snow, we can rub it
all over to make our pictures fresh.

After this comes February,
month after month of staying inside the lines.
Now at least we can say it is snow
that makes our art unfinished.
We have saved this white crayon
like a virgin for thirty-one days,
relying instead on nothing and a Wedgewood sky.

WORDS LIKE MONKEYS

Words like monkeys belong in a cage.
There they sit on stick swings
and eat bananas, covering the floor
with crushed daffodils.
They smile, their teeth are marble palaces.
They wrap their knuckles around the bars,
shake, shriek, think of freedom, weep.

The smallest word is I.
It is my favorite, anyway,
dark-eyed and practically quiet.
If I tuck in my serifs
I am slender enough
to slip the bars,
stand beyond the gate.
So this is how it feels when air
moves without stripes.
I am released, run free

all the way to your cage.
You sit ignoring evil,
three-lettered in a bulk,
an over-ripe banana in hand.
You, you call me, changing my name.
Your fingers cross a world apart,
splatter mine between the metal bars,
find my hair nested with sweat.
This is as far as I can go
after hopping into exhaustion
from the wish to stand close

to you. Words are our bodies,
and what I have to say
is locked in every cell,
soaking in one woman's blood,
nothing you have ever heard,
primitive, beneath you.

PENITENTS

Brother John also suffered on my account.
This was a long time ago, before I knew you,
before I was born, when love was still new.

He was peeling fruit in the abbey's kitchen
when the thought of me provoked a hunger
he knew he couldn't control. You understand.

They had ways of dealing with those things then.
Public, within their small group. I was there
only in his mind, a guilty witness.

He knelt on stone and potsherd, soon red,
as friends obliged him his bit of shame.
We agreed it was for everyone's good.

Perhaps your wife has a few old dishes
she is willing to crash upon the floor.
How silly you would look bleeding a little

as she and I took turns scourging
your soft shoulders with our rods.
You would whimper, too proud to howl,

and let us know you were hurting more
than any woman who ever fell beneath desire.
John said the same thing, I remember now,

before he stumbled from the chapel,
weeping at the discovery that pain hurts
and hurts, and nothing more.

WRITING ON ANOTHER PERSON'S BIRTHDAY

It is impossible to imagine someone else's day.
Years ago a man began the long march
across continents in death's slow cartage.
Today he looks at the calendar as if to say
it makes no difference, on a day like the rest
I robbed my mother of her singularity,
I broke off a piece of her life and slipped
into the blue and white light of existence
to begin the search for my own.

Maybe that isn't what today's person would say.
When I write for him, I take the pen from his hand
and wrap it around mine. I claim for him
skin and the color of the sky when he was born.
I predict for him resignation at his years
and the silent relinquishing of his secret dream.
Like the mother deported far from his touch,
I take him back, hold him in my hands,
shape him for a moment to my incomplete
        and miraculous conception.

FIRST CLASS

The instructor moves to the front of the room
with a stomach full of blood.
She sees a field of faces waiting for something;
one of her eyes falls forward, hits the desk,
splattering light in their direction.

They do not know she has second sight,
that they sit in chairs already filled
the best ever by the first class.
She sees them, a ghost to every chair,
a weird wizard forever strolling into view
and past, so far gone that time
is a distance only astronomers know.

She knows her life can never be the same again,
fool in front of like fools, fool
giving herself away like precious goods.
When she looks up at the clock,
the night is gone. When she looks at the year,
she knows her heart is gone. When she sees them again,
she will say: you will soon learn
that I cannot love you a second time.

LAKEWOOD CENTER

I am standing out in the hall while my students evaluate their
        instructor.
I try not to feel their pencils, I try
not to ask how many more times I can do this.
The Hatha Yoga class left weeks ago, chanting
        I am free I am free,
silly women with leotards compressing their breasts,
so tonight all I hear is the computer room, tap-tap,
        click and spit.
At the far end of the building, a place for all kinds of people,
a doorway of light reveals that dog obedience still meets
week after week like we do week after week.
Once a black dachshund failed to skim a six inch hurdle
and was yanked sharply for his feckless leap.
I saw his eyes darken and thought, I could love him
as no one else, not like the lady on the end of the leash.
If he were mine, I would let him hug the ground forever.
If my students were poets, they would write:
she stood in the hall and looked at the rest of her life,
and then she came back to us and we discussed
        Chapter Sixteen.

MIRAGE

A man said he would go find spring on the other side
of the world, or at least in Arizona, a dish of sand.
The sky would open like a drawer
and out fall flowers, blooming ulcers
on a sapless landscape.
Actually , that's not what he said,
but he's going anyway with a kaleidoscope
in mind: symmetry, color, and rocks.

Past midnight, if that counts as tomorrow,
I rose from bed and went into the other room
imitating a specter of love.
The window shone like a rare white beast
from a brief swirl of snow.
I lay down again in the light without any light,
what snow makes from the fallout of stars.
He was asleep by then, holding cacti by the waist
and dancing every bit as good as his dreams.
He will go there and know the lack of water,
return before this snow has joined the ground.
I will sleep better when his travel is complete,
when the sand has washed itself free of his hair
and I am the one the sun finds
casting shadows across his eyes.

CASTAWAY

Somewhere there is an island of your perfect understanding.
We have all seen the cartoonist's lone palm,
a dome of sand and sun and sea.
I sit hunched in rags
dressed in time
thirsty
bookless in that one tree's shade
and envious of gulls.
As an act of mercy towards my long life
someone may sketch in a bobbing bottle,
something at last for me to read,
or when I pop the cork
you flow out instead and stand
a genie, a sultan, a rescuer
to share what has always been my space:
it could be.
I stand knee-deep in milky waves
reaching for you
day after day.
The horizon has become a line
bisecting my eyes,
half of me always waiting.
Whose island is this? you ask
as you walk upon the water.
Is what confines you
big enough for two?
I have those answers here in my hands,
in these conch shells
continuously assenting.

AN ALMOST HAPPY BIRTHDAY

Dizzy from so many trips around the sun
you stop
two days before all pretense of youth
falls away, the smooth skin you will never again wear.
I am sorry you are old before I ever knew
how scared you were as a boy.
That is what you still understand about all of us,
how scared we were as children,
the boy in you who has not died.

Graying, creasing, slowing down
(as you whirl once more around the sun
I wish you many returns of the day)
you stop
young for the last time
stupefied at how long it's been
since your parents accidentally threw you
away from themselves
into your own orbit
(it was not far enough to free you
from the fear of terrible collisions)
where you continue to drift
like a small stick mid-stream
and provoke (I see)
these widening circles.

LADY CRANE

She sails down into the brackish water
of a brook run low at summer's end.
Still, she is a woman by instinct
and never lets the water lap
above her reedy legs, touch
the space where eggs fell from
her body like unwelcome gifts.
For years she has walked downstream
to defy extinction so that
today she can stand in the sun
listening to the cattails cry
with the wind and the tall grass.
Her neck becomes a bare root
bracing a tree against the shore.
She can stand still forever.
Or walk spastically, head swiveling
blinking and dipping for dinner.
Gray wings buckle and fold
close to where her arms would be
ready to reach for the sun.
She knows who stands watching
in a flowering sheer dress.
A few long steps remove her
from women who pause at their work
and with a quick jerk of the head
beg the beauty no one else sees.

BREATHING ON MIRRORS

Under the snow the ground holds a silver honeycomb
of ice locked in from autumn rain, while
I am trying to count on all my fingers the times
I rose from bed with nothing else but the thought
that I was the only one who knew what I knew

and who like someone without a pulse, someone
who wears the squint of summer year-round,
a person palsied from the tasks of life,
needs the help of a small mirror, raw at the edges,

the kind women used to carry in handbags to check
the oily red ghosts at their mouths, a mirror
not to show me who I am, like a photo snapped
to save my sitting on a rock knees bent with love

far past any useful reminder of what I lost,
but held up with effrontery before my face
to catch my spirit leaving with the next exhale
as proof that I have not disappeared into

other people's stories, but still live miraculously here,
where I obscure over and over with thin clouds
and disbelief in the tiniest condensation
an off-balance view of my beautiful face.

GOD

Forget Jehovah, a god bigger than the sky.
The one you want, the one most of America listens for,
is small and sleek as a marble statue
set upon a mantle of fine wood.
You admire it for the smooth craft and design
that make you know the feel of it in your hand
as surely as if you had warmed it in your pocket.
Actually, he's a little bigger than that,
a graceful man from the Mediterranean
but more the north shore type, French or Italian,
the kind of person you would find running a gallery
where only quality works are set out.
If you came into his place he would let you wander,
then approach you with a smile.
The smell of linen and fresh air rise from him,
offensive to nobody, certainly not you.
Just looking, but he knew that all along.
His eyes point to the painting you have already chosen
as best out of everything in the room:
its color and form confirm what you know is right.
There is so much beauty in the world that he goes off
to talk to someone else entering through the door,
but his glances follow you around the room.
It is then that you know you will never leave.
He is still in front of the door where you would have to ask
please for his slight body to step aside,
and it will be tomorrow before you have to go.
Instead you take him from the mantle
with your right hand and hold him
so tightly that you hear his voice.

THIS

BID PRAYER

First I ask what I should ask to ask.
The simplest things aren't always clear.

Immediately I enter Land of Paradox.
Unworthy I get grace.
Frail I bear the load of life.
Blessed I return begging.

Figure it out for me, Triple Lord.
Oxidize my words to flame
as smoky thoughts sting my eyes
and concentration wanes.

Without meaning to I rhyme.
Words that rise must find beauty
and a shape wrought by ancient seers.
I falter, then I start.

In a voice no one hears I offer this:
amplify my spirit
however small, unraveling rag, white flag,
make me a saintly tablecloth or pall.
More.
Compared to what I asked before
I ask to ask for more.

ABOUT MY PAST LIVES

I know I must have come first of all from China
so long ago that I was smaller than a horde.
Wearing silky rags of solitude I wandered
without stopping north and west to the steppes
where I suffered for centuries, telling about it
in cyrillic with softly trilled r's.
When I remember those days it's like reading a book
backward without seeing the title page first,
knowing only the waterfall of chapters about everyone else
who brought me here to the high-tech corridor of Illinois,
and the burden of walking as far as the sun
after all those impossibly antique nights
spent close to the Wall, the golden domes, this corn
so many times harvested.

WALKING IN THE RAIN

I become the leopard,
and as a cat fear these sudden spots
smacking my cheeks, my flank.
They have fallen so far to find me
bringing a smell that was not here before,
the scent of asphalt griddle mixed with grass
or the sweet dust of heaven.
I try to think: pennies, kisses, chocolate drops
plunking on my head and shoulders,
oozing through my clothes.
From this I will thicken into willow
unless, if ahead the light grows clearer,
I dry off under an apricot sky.

ESCAPE

Right now every poem I read is a lie.
The true story of what poets do with life
remains unheard, lost in the sound of traffic,
the door swallowed shut, a velvet eye averted.
They have written none of this nor explained
how day is squeezed into the crack called midnight,
how we refuse to admit we can't fly.
The ear of the poet is shaped like a shell
where a dumb animal works to get out.
Its escape will not make itself known.
You will not hear it when it leaves,
its silence having become similar to your own.

DREAD

Walking home on the Fourth of July
I try to imagine being free.
From the sky I pull images born on air:
sandpipers, smoke, and ancient starlight.
But each step takes me back to a mausoleum
where darkness hunkers in a black hole.
My address is a place I don't want to be,
the man and I become a crowd,
chairs arranged in concrete.

Speeding down the road in a red car
an arm reaches out through the window
as if to wave hello to me,
but like some sick Liberty her torch
spits a dizzy flare past my ear.
My shoulders rise, a cape about my head,
and Queen Anne's lace shivers.
Let me lie down a minute in this quiet ditch
where water no longer flows
so I can feel earth sinking
like an endless featherbed.

DISTURBED GROUND

Caught between fields of corn (green lunatic fringe)
knee-high to Goliath in early July
and macadam mile after mile
(forced to bear us, pressed into place
to spare us life in the mud)
grow most of my favorites:
chicory (a blue stolen from purple)
sweet clover (yielding secrets to bees)
lace from Queen Anne's old gowns
day lilies (open beaks before they shrivel)
broken Budweiser bottles bejeweling the sun
with their fluted caps half full of rain
and gravel, just gravel scattered among the roots
where I walk past and marvel
at what holds up the sky

17 JULY

At the crack of dawn Day rose
and reached for something to wear,
cotton polished dark as stone
with a ripple of marble or milk.
I can do this again, he said to his woman,
good-bye, my lady, usurper of dreams,
then yawned like a fish and flashed
the bright button of the sun through every bound hole.
She wrapped herself in robes of shadow
as he took his place in the summer sky
like a man who every morning gets up
proud of his fresh blue shirt,
one of many.

SIGHTING THE DEER

The rain has eased to a slight drizzle;
we have eaten and gone out looking for deer in the gloom.
Across an open field three of them appear grazing,
junior in the middle, a tree on top of dad's head,
prudence wrinkling the soft skin above the mother's eye.
She sees us first and lets us know how far away they stand
on legs thinner than the bones of uneaten grass,
her ribs playing a flute we cannot hear.
We have destroyed the peace of their family dinner
as a briefly freed ray of sun brightens their coats
to a brown warmer than sand along a creek.
Over and over we remark on the miracle that they are there
until our chorus of praise at their surprising beauty
tickles the silk of their ears and they spin
with tails lifted to light three white candles
extinguished by flight, forest, and mutual sorrow.

SEPTEMBER STORY

Once you walked into the house that tried to kill you
and looked out the window at a dome of red sumacs
as beautiful as anything you have ever seen:
you thought everything would start to get better.
It did, or at least you lived through that winter
as the seasons fell all over themselves and brought you back
to September so you could watch a good friend die.
Now, two years later, you realize you ignored the date
and never thought to leave clover on her sweet grave.
Time—Mr. Great Healer—please don't let me forget
ten thousand lovely early autumns from now
to remember the park with the yellow sun in the yellow air
or the night I drove faster than a waxing moon,
how the asters grace the field like an old man's fallen hair
or that I am so afraid I will never feel like this
happily ever after in the cool sunshine again.
The sumacs would look this way without me.
The sun is an enormous red ball to the very end.

IN THE DARK

This early wet autumn night—
this stupid evening when I went to the library
and came out into a rain too brief to wash
the dust off the sidewalks or polish up the leaves—
I got in my car thinking about how I could die
without ever tasting a man again.
Why won't that stop sign gleam at the corner,
why do I have to know from forty thousand other trips
that it is there so some guy won't ram me?
A factory and parking lot fall away behind,
I'm driving in the harvest darkness going home.
In fact I am invisible, underwater, impossible to see
without my headlights on. No wonder night closed in.
My left hand that is forever dropping lids and soapy jars
spins a lever—aah—one executed thought can light my way.
I can do anything, pierce the road with yellow bands
and set the next stop sign on fire.
If I had to, I could have walked all this way
even through the rain. Or crawled.
Or convinced myself that being in the dark is easy.
Good thinking, I hand myself the praise.
The books I got become a tower stacked beside my bed.

THE FIRST LITTLE PIG

It wasn't such a bad idea, almost pre-fab
sitting there in a shorn field looking like a house
just about big enough for me.
I scooped out the insides and ate them
while my sisters fussed with sticks and bricks,
then made a scratchy bed to lie on
and admired my strawberry tummy.
When he knocked I just kept on humming,
and the straw, glued by rain and sun,
would have kept out any vandal.
What they've got wrong in the story
is that it really was a whole pack
pressing at my door like a veritable plague
of marauders from the land of Khan.
That night they howled till my earflaps tingled
and I was ready to turn myself in for bacon.
They never said what they wanted, why my
pink flesh would taste so sweet stripped from the bone,
what amusement my squeal provoked for what purpose
except power. I refused to point to my smarter sisters.
When their foul wolf breath huffed as they puffed
and blew my stalks down, I was left standing
stupid, the story would make you believe,
not as pretty as walled-in pig number three.
But they came for me first and not just because
I was easy. I never thought about hiding,
which is how I met them and the world,
their long teeth shadowed in the winter sun.
Who I was naked, with a halo of chaff blowing free,
is what finally drove them away.

BLOODLESS

Today when the doctor poked me to find blood
all he did was make holes in the nook of my arm.
I felt like a fool because my veins roll
and take with them what feeds my body
so I don't dry up into a walking raisin.
But he didn't get even one ruby drop from me.
I have it all, a full tank, my clanging chambers full
except for what the vampire got last night
with his siphoning smile and something
that felt so much like a kiss I could have sworn
it was only morning's last shadow.
You check my outsides while I look within
just to make sure I am nothing but pink.
Maybe my blood is just shy,
blushing between heartbeats and hiding from men,
blue in its only revelation.
I listen to it pound on the doors of my head, my chest,
and stand breathless from the effort to explain
how I can be this empty miracle.

trust

dizzy from one taste of harvest fields
a thousand dark birds settle on the road.
there they eat macadam and rest their wings
testing their luck car by car,
or else these birdbrains harbor trust:
armless, they let her take the wheel.
when she honks they will rise up like gnats.
they will not grace her foreign grill.
a beaded glance tells them she approaches
as they gather into a dry black cloud.
some of them will never make it if
they stay to watch the end.

she is human she is woman she is earth
and writes only what she knows.

pushing aside her grackle-spattered cape
she lifts a hand to clear the road.

PRAYING FOR THE DEAD

Theologically there is no reason to stick with the living. The
    dead
were God's children too before their bones got piled up to the
    clouds
after they worked on their loins so we'd be here. May they
rest in peace, may they r i p, may they
intercede for us, mayday, mayday.

It could be your whole life before you recall all their names
and invoke His blessing on their crumbling heads.
While you remember them to the last stillborn child,
take time to intercede for your own dead selves:
the baby post-World War II, the schoolchild of new suburbia,
the student running her fingers over pages of Shelley,
and the bride—oh say a special prayer for the bride
who fumbles with her buttons and steps out of her shroud,
who too many years later hears her own voice pleading
as she tries to bestow on her life one word of grace.

FLESH

As a little blond girl I knew
the white crayon made a ghost of my self-portrait
while the pink made me blush like a bunny.
Band-aids too salmon
and my grandma's stockings the color of pumpkin mush
were more evidence of an imperfect world
and the mystery of skin.

Then I discovered how blackberry brambles
could only snag the surface, tear the net
and in a few days I'd be smooth.
When I cut the butter with the wrong knife,
my hand opened like more butter
releasing blood I could understand.

Now I know I am made of more parts
than there are stars in the sky.
I am arranged inside a slip-cover
that bears a yellow tinge from Mongols
whose bodies were smashed like cups
after delicious drinking.
They dried up and fell from their bones
in a way I cannot imagine doing.
Because they were flesh,
I take up my pencil and hold it
like a lover, feel it dent
my first knuckle and give pleasure.

THE DISTANCE OF STARS

Even from here where I stick out like a thorn
on the side of a bumpy green planet
it looks like too far to live, too close for dying.
Strings of stars stretch from one star
to the next: nothing is measured by belief.
They will never implode into harmless disaster.
Stars shine, and everything else stays silent.
I raise my hand to judge the darkness,
covering one gap with the width of a finger.
In the same way I can measure what separates
my wide leonine eyes.
Between blinking I pretend to know
how heaven bridges the earthly to the sublime.

IN DECEMBER

Here's what you need to do to crack open December.
Take an ax, swing, bury it up to the handle
in the mud of a still unfrozen field.
The land was textured with the season's first snow
and now you have made a short brown mark
to be proud of. From those putty lips
up flies a varied flock of doves, turning their wings
now gray now white in the direction of the hidden sun.
You set them free to taste winter.
If you want to fly instead of climbing up ladders
go over there where you were fortunate to see them.
Kneel. Become a clod. Don an icy shell.
When someone tiptoes up behind you
the swish will barely warn you of the thud.
Don't scream. Words will emerge more directly
from your cleaved skull if your eyes as they roll
stay open (winter, is it still winter?)
to glimpse their rising like diamond flakes
to form one enormous cloud.

BEGGAR

In desperation I try outer space.
It's bound to be different than mudball Earth,
and it is: not empty black, but white as a glowing cloud.
I feel like I'm breathing mist except I start gasping.
Then I am begging and one of my former lives
calls to mind Bombay where everyone walking by spat
and I was grateful enough to call it rain.

Please, even the smallest coin or scraps of beef
preferably with the fat left on. A cookie for dessert?
Our ebony spaceship etches the enormous sky.
I think I'm sprawled in a leather seat
or else this is luxury's gutter.
Having risen so far by my own power, I reach
for one speck of stardust, its diamond light
spraying beauty off the lip of my tin can cup.
Bless you, and this token.

SWANS OF WINTER

In the elbow of the creek
winter wears her white sleeve:
powder, mist, and bleaching sun
hang veils between the banks of snow
that part their lips for flowing water.
And there like apparitions from a fairy time
two swans float, exhale perfumed steam,
discuss the survival of love at zero
and delineate for morning's traveler
pale shapes with no background
as their necks wave and catch
on frozen swallows.

THE FAR COUNTRY

Luke 15:13

What I remember most is not the desert lands
where I lost more than my money
or the lakes that seemed to have fallen from the sky
but the incredible sense of space:
between stars
between small bits of sand
between my two eyes
where stretching out on all sides as far as I could tell
there was nobody
except me.

I found my wisdom under rocks.
At dusk the snaking songs released by flutes
became straight as vectors piercing my chest.
I watched the planets move
and come morning fed the pigs.
I discovered what it was to be their master.

The space, already infinite, expanded over time.
I spent all of it making paths
that led to imaginary cities.
Once a bird flew on past me;
I longed to give it just one wing.

My leisure became the silken tent of despair,
a place to rest from the heat of the day
and hide from the closed eye of night.
It billowed like the lungs of an old man.
I kept trying to breathe out, breathe out.

No one wants to hear a story which has no
middle. For years nothing happened.
And in spite of what others may tell you,
I did not mourn the house I had forsaken
thinking it was not mine.
I remained convinced there was no place like home.

The ending is what you are waiting for,
my account of the moment truth closed in
and with human hands shook me
to wake me up, to point me back down the road.
But what I remember is that it was not that way.
I am who I am is a slow piece of poem to write.
It is so close to life that we must almost die
before we write the first word.

Let the first word, then, be mystery,
because I do not know how I made my way back.
But when he held me at the gate I felt his heart beat
so fast clasped like fingers between the beating of my own—
no drum ever so continuous, no gaps, no space—
that I felt the claustrophobia of his love
as if I had never traveled far apart for so long
or wasted this much time alone.

COMING ALONG

Last night's dream in which I set out to hurt my daughter
turns out not to be close to what I do.
She falls so far away from the pull of my body
where once I wrapped around her like the moon
that my hand kept slipping her wrist
and the words that would have diced her heart
broke into shapeless pieces with the six o'clock sun.
As a woman she will do better than me.
Her breasts will tilt like morning glories to his gaze,
her fingers learn to separate clinging from their letting go.
My mess will be her garden, and I'll find comfort
to see her tending the next row.
What I dreamed last night does not deserve telling;
because I had a nightmare it can't come true.
Writing these few lines will help both of us practice
the magic trick of slow continuous being before
she joins me in this life of blood and truth.

LEAPING

Despair is my old mother;
I was sired from a cold eye.

Birth cut me free
to flounder in my seeking.

They remarked on my taciturnity
though the cellar teemed with words.

Now that I am grown up on the plains
I am about to lose everything.

Threshed and bare I wait
for gravity's comfort.

First I lift my hand
to find a synonym for dance.

I become my own gift, self-giver,
in gratitude and leaping.